MERCURY

by L. L. Owens

The Child's World®

Published by The Child's World®
1980 Lookout Drive • Mankato, MN 56003-1705
800-599-READ • www.childsworld.com

ACKNOWLEDGMENTS
The Child's World®: Mary Berendes, Publishing Director
The Design Lab: Design and production
Red Line Editorial: Editorial direction

PHOTO CREDITS
AP Images, cover, 1, 32; NASA/courtesy of nasaimages.org, cover, 1, 3,
6, 12, 15, 18, 19, 24, 26, 27, 31; Ed Darack/Corbis, 5; NASA/courtesy of
nasaimages.org/The Design Lab, 6, 7; Arturbo/iStockphoto, 9; AP Images/
The Design Lab, 11; NASA Jet Propulsion Laboratory (NASA-JPL), 13, 17, 21,
23, 29; Steffen Foerster/iStockphoto, 25

LIBRARY OF CONGRESS CATALOGING-IN-PUBLICATION DATA
Owens, L. L.
 Mercury / by L.L. Owens.
  p. cm.
 Includes bibliographical references and index.
 ISBN 978-1-60954-384-6 (library bound : alk. paper)
 1. Mercury (Planet)—Juvenile literature. I. Title.
 QB611.O94 2011
 523.41—dc22

                                2010039961

Printed in the United States of America
Mankato, MN
December, 2012
PA02160

ON THE COVER
The spacecraft *Messenger*
took this image of Mercury.
The planet is gray, but the
orange coloring highlights
its uneven surface.

Table of Contents

Mercury and the Solar System

Try looking near the sun just before sunrise or sunset. Do you see a second bright object in the sky? That's Mercury!

Mercury is one of our space neighbors in the **solar system**. At the center of our solar system is the sun. Planets go around, or **orbit**, the sun.

Mercury (top) can often be seen in the sky at dawn. Venus is to the left of the moon.

5

SUN

Mercury
Venus
Earth
Mars
Ceres
Jupiter

Fun Facts

PLANET NUMBER: Mercury is the first planet from the sun.

DISTANCE FROM SUN: 36 million miles (58 million km)

SIZE: The distance around Mercury's middle is about 9,525 miles (15,329 km). That's longer than 100 million hot dogs placed end to end!

OUR SOLAR SYSTEM: Our solar system has eight planets and five dwarf planets. Pluto used to be called a planet. But in 2006, scientists decided to call it a dwarf planet instead. Scientists hope to discover even more dwarf planets in our solar system!

Our Solar System

Saturn

Uranus

Neptune

Pluto

Haumea

Makemake

Eris

━●━ **Planet**

━●━ *Dwarf Planet*

More than 2,000 years ago, Romans studied the night sky. They noticed one bright object moving faster than the others. They named it after one of their gods—Mercury. That god was the fastest of all.

Mercury is often called the Swift Planet. Its orbit around the sun takes only 88 Earth days. One full orbit equals one year. It takes Earth about 365 days to orbit the sun once!

Mercury was the Roman god of roads and travel.

9

While orbiting the sun, a planet spins like a top. Each planet spins, or rotates, on an invisible line called an **axis**. It runs through the planet from top to bottom. One rotation equals one day. Think of one day on a planet as the time from one sunrise to the next sunrise.

Mercury rotates very slowly. It rotates on its axis once every 59 Earth days. An Earth day is 24 hours. That means one day on Mercury is 1,416 hours!

An axis runs through the center of a planet. The planet spins on the axis.

A Hard, Rocky Planet

Some planets are rocky and hard, and others are made of **gas** with no hard surface. Mercury is a **terrestrial** planet. Mercury has mountains, canyons, and volcanoes.

Fun Fact

There are two types of planets.

TERRESTRIAL PLANETS (mostly rock) are close to the sun. They are: Mercury, Venus, Earth, and Mars.

GAS GIANTS (mostly gas and liquid) are farther from the sun. They are: Jupiter, Saturn, Uranus, and Neptune.

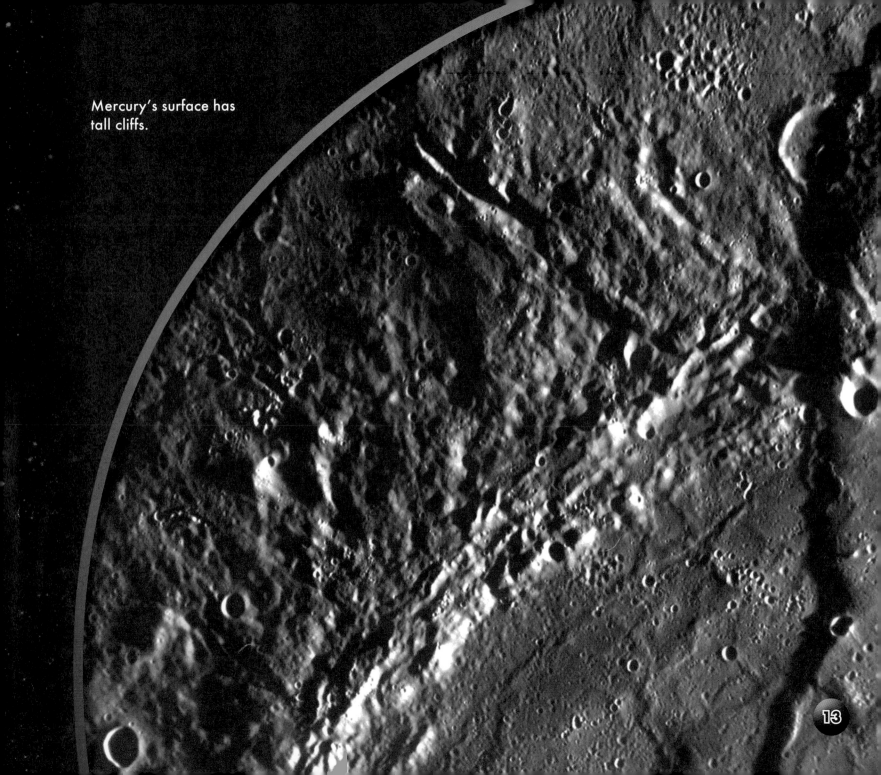

Mercury's surface has
tall cliffs.

13

A Closer Look

Mercury looks like Earth's moon. It is dark gray. Its surface is covered in thick dust. Millions of years ago, **asteroids** hit Mercury. The broken rocks formed that dust. The asteroids also created many deep **craters**.

Earth's moon has craters, like Mercury. Humans first walked on the moon in 1969.

Mercury's Caloris Basin is one of the largest craters in the solar system. It is about 800 miles (1,300 km) across. That is about the length of the state of California!

But Mercury has some plains, or flat areas, too. Volcanoes erupted on Mercury millions of years ago. Those volcanoes spewed red-hot **lava**. The lava filled craters and flowed across the land. Mercury's plains formed as it cooled and hardened.

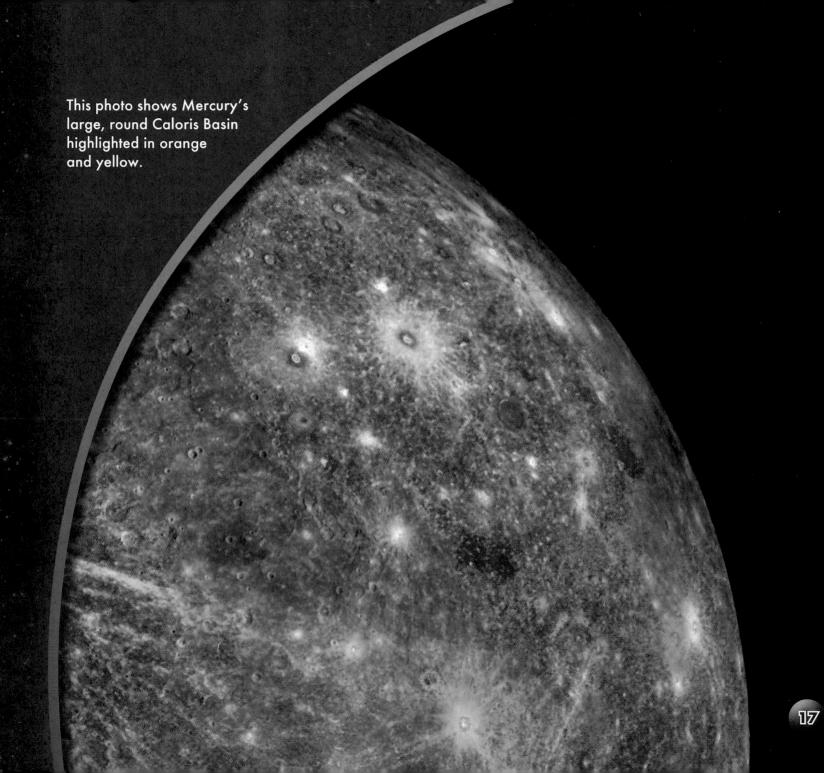

This photo shows Mercury's large, round Caloris Basin highlighted in orange and yellow.

Weather and Water

Because Mercury is so close to the sun, the planet gets very hot during the day. A high temperature on Mercury can be more than 800°F (425°C). That is about six times as hot as Earth's hottest desert!

But Mercury gets cold at night. A nighttime low can sink to nearly −300°F (−185°C).

The sun is a star that is believed to be more than 4 billion years old.

19

A planet's **atmosphere** is the layer of gas around it. Earth's atmosphere is the air that we breathe. Mercury's atmosphere is very thin. The sun's heat makes Mercury's gases quickly disappear into space. No clouds form. There is no rain or wind. The sky is pitch black, except for stars.

In 2008, the *Messenger* spacecraft took this picture of Mercury. The spacecraft studied Mercury's surface and atmosphere.

All life as we know it needs water. So scientists try to find water on other planets. They once thought Mercury didn't have any. Now they believe ice exists deep in some craters near Mercury's northern **pole**. The sun's heat would boil away any water on the surface. But the bottoms of those northern craters see almost no sunlight.

Ice might exist in Mercury's north pole craters.

Exploring the Planet

How do scientists know about Mercury? No one has ever walked on the planet. But scientists have sent spacecraft to explore it. Scientists use strong **telescopes** to observe Mercury from Earth.

Fun Fact

Because of its high temperatures, Mercury is hard to study. The closest a spacecraft got to Mercury was still 142 miles (229 km) from the planet's surface. That's about the same as looking at Philadelphia from Washington DC!

These large space telescopes and observatories are in Hawaii.

25

In 2004, NASA launched the spacecraft *Messenger* to fly near Mercury. It took exciting pictures of the planet's surface. We will soon have a full map of the planet.

Fun Fact

NASA stands for the National Aeronautics and Space Administration. It is a US agency that studies space and the planets.

Messenger prepares to launch from Cape Canaveral Air Force Station in 2004.

In the future, NASA hopes to get new **data** about the planet's size, structure, and history. That will help us better understand Mercury and how our solar system came to be.

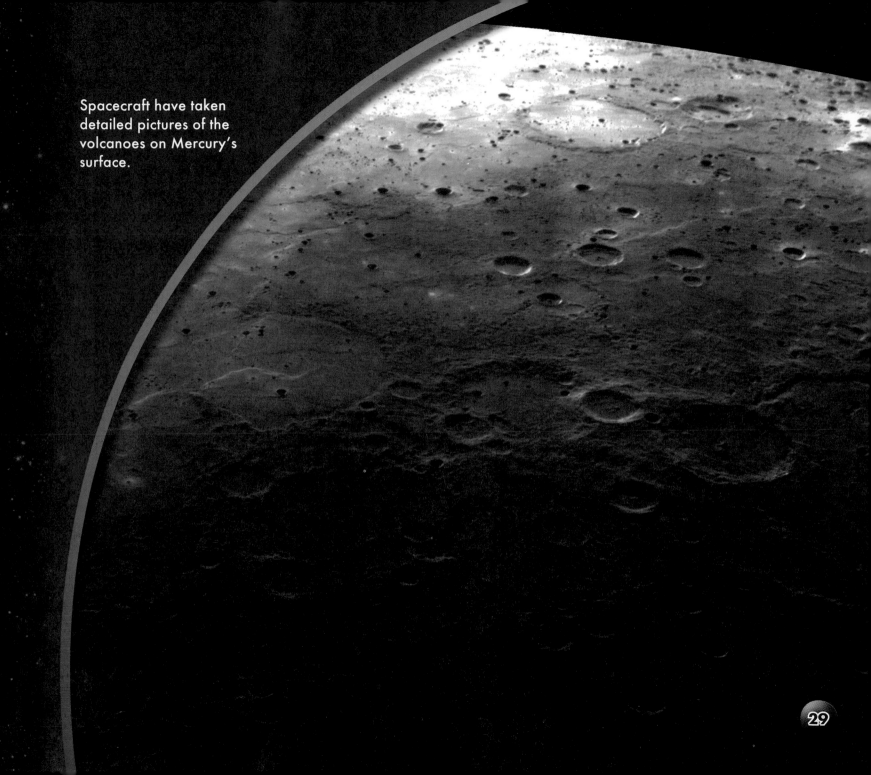

Spacecraft have taken detailed pictures of the volcanoes on Mercury's surface.

GLOSSARY

asteroids (ASS-tuh-roidz): Asteroids are rocks that orbit the sun. Asteroids caused craters on Mercury's surface.

atmosphere (AT-muhss-fihr): An atmosphere is the mixture of gases around a planet or a star. Mercury has a thin atmosphere.

axis (AK-siss): An axis is an imaginary line that runs through the center of a planet or a moon. Mercury rotates on its axis.

craters (KRAY-turz): Craters are large areas on the surface of a moon or a planet that dip down, like bowls. Mercury has many craters on its surface.

data (DAY-tuh): Data are facts, figures, and other information. Scientists hope to learn more data about Mercury.

dwarf planets (DWORF PLAN-itz): Dwarf planets are round bodies in space that orbit the sun, are not moons, and are not large enough to clear away their paths around the sun. Dwarf planets often have similar objects that orbit near them.

gas (GASS): A gas is a substance that moves around freely and can spread out. Some planets are made mostly of gas.

lava (LAH-vuh): Lava is molten, or melted, rock from a volcano or a deep crack in land. Hardened lava on Mercury's surface forms plains.

observatories (uhb-ZUR-vuh-tor-eez): Observatories are places with telescopes and other tools for studying space. Observatories allow scientists to study Mercury from Earth.

orbit (OR-bit): To orbit is to travel around another body in space, often in an oval path. Planets orbit the sun.

pole (POHL): A pole is either of two endpoints on a planet or a moon's axis of rotation. Scientists believe water is in the craters near Mercury's north pole.

solar system (SOH-lur SISS-tum): Our solar system is made up of the sun, eight planets and their moons, and smaller bodies that orbit the sun. Mercury is the first planet from the sun in our solar system.

telescopes (TEL-uh-skohps): Telescopes are tools for making faraway objects appear closer. Scientists study Mercury using telescopes.

terrestrial (tuh-RESS-tree-uhl): Terrestrial describes planets that have firm land, like Earth. Mercury is a terrestrial planet.

FURTHER INFORMATION

BOOKS

Colligan, L. H. *Mercury*. New York: Marshall Cavendish Benchmark, 2009.

Landau, Elaine. *Mercury*. Danbury, CT: Children's Press, 2008.

Trammel, Howard K. *The Solar System*. New York: Children's Press, 2010.

WEB SITES

Visit our Web site for links about Mercury: **childsworld.com/links**

Note to Parents, Teachers, and Librarians: We routinely verify our Web links to make sure they are safe and active sites. So encourage your readers to check them out!

INDEX

ABOUT THE AUTHOR

L. L. Owens has been writing books for children since 1998. She writes both fiction and nonfiction and especially loves helping kids explore the world around them.